# SOLIDS, LIQUIDS AND GASES

Linda Howe

Collins Educational

*An imprint of HarperCollinsPublishers*

# Acknowledgements

Copyright © 1991 Linda Howe
ISBN 0 00 317588 X
Published by Collins Educational
*An imprint of* HarperCollins*Publishers*
77-85 Fulham Palace Road
London W6 8JB

Reprinted 1994, 1997

Design by Shireen Nathoo
Illustrations by Helen Herbert (Graham-Cameron
Illustration), Sally Neave and Gay Galsworthy
Cover illustration by Debi Ani
Commissioned photography by Oliver Hatch

Typeset by Kalligraphic Design Ltd., Horley, Surrey
Printed and bound in Hong Kong

The publishers thank Beyton County Middle School,
Suffolk and Fielding Middle School, London for their
kind co-operation in the production of Collins Primary
Science.

Photographs - The publishers would like to thank the
following for permission to reproduce photographs:

The J Allan Cash Photolibrary 12(t), 15, 23, 28 (b), 38,
43x3; London Fire Brigade 35(b); Mary Evans Picture
Library 20(t); Robert Harding Picture Library 20(c), 28(c).

t = top, b = bottom, c = centre, l = left, r = right

# Contents

# HELPFUL NOTES

In these books you will be:

★ trying out ideas

★ seeing what you can find out

★ making and using models

★ using different ways to show what you find out

Look out for these signs and they will help you.

**ACTIVITY**

This sign is at the beginning of each activity.
The activities give you ideas for things you can make, things you can try and ways of finding things out.

**COLLECT**

This sign tells you what you need to collect before you begin an activity. Things that you might need are shown in the box. If you can't find all the things in the list think of other things in your classroom that you could use instead. Remember that we just give you ideas for materials to use. You may need to find other things so that you can try out your own ideas.

**OTHER IDEAS**

This sign asks you to think of ideas of your own.
Always talk your ideas over with a friend as they can usually help you with your thinking.
Before you try a test of your own, plan it carefully.
Remember these things:

1. Think about what you want to make, try, or find out.
2. Collect what you need.
3. Try out your ideas. Can you improve them in any way?
4. Record what you have done.

It is important to work safely and carefully. Sometimes, when you are using tools or handling hot things, you will need to take special care. This sign tells you when to take extra care.

**FIND OUT**

When you see this sign you will need to find things out for yourself.

You will need to decide how to find out what you need. You may need to:

- ▶ look in some books from the library
- ▶ write some letters
- ▶ ask other people
- ▶ look closely at some pictures, the television or a video.

**RECORD**

When you are doing an activity you will need to think about how you will show what you find out. Sometimes you will need to choose a way that will help you remember what you have done and sometimes you will need to choose a way that will tell other people what you have found out. There are lots of ways of recording your activities. Here are some for you to choose from:

- ▶ making a chart, graph or table
- ▶ writing a list
- ▶ drawing a picture
- ▶ taking a photograph
- ▶ keeping notes while you are working
- ▶ making a tape recording
- ▶ using a computer fact file
- ▶ writing about what you have done

# 1 WHAT IS A LIQUID?

Water is a liquid. Like other liquids, water:
- ▶ has no shape of its own
- ▶ finds its own level
- ▶ and is runny.

Liquids take the shape of the container they are in.
What is happening here?

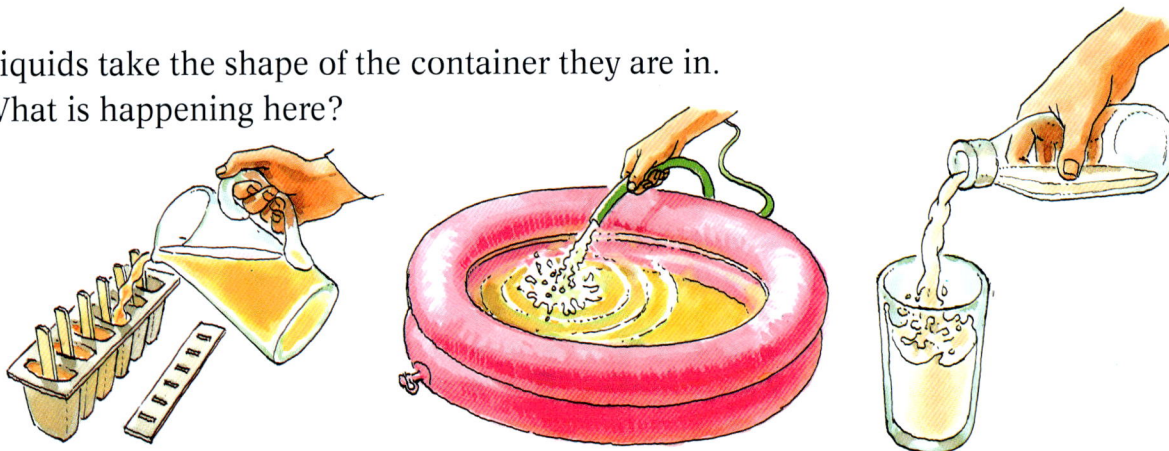

Can you say what happens to the shape of the water when:

the baby's bath is
filled from the taps?

the baby fills a toy
with water?

the baby splashes water
onto the floor?

Make a list of the liquids you use.
Make a coloured mark next to the
liquids which you feel are most
important to you.

Liquids I use

| | |
|---|---|
| Water | Petrol |
| tea | Orange |
| coffee | coke |
| Washing-up liquid | milk |
| liquid soap | beer |
| bubble bath | gravy |
| Paint | glue |
| Shampoo | tipex |
| ink | |

# Liquids always find their own level

COLLECT

FOOD COLOUR BLUE

FOOD COLOUR RED

Plastic containers with screw-on tops  •  food colourings

## ACTIVITY – A –

Put a little food colouring in each container and half fill them with water. Put the tops on the containers and stand them on a flat surface. Look at the water levels. Draw what you see.

Lay the containers on their sides. What has happened to the levels of the water? Draw what you see now.

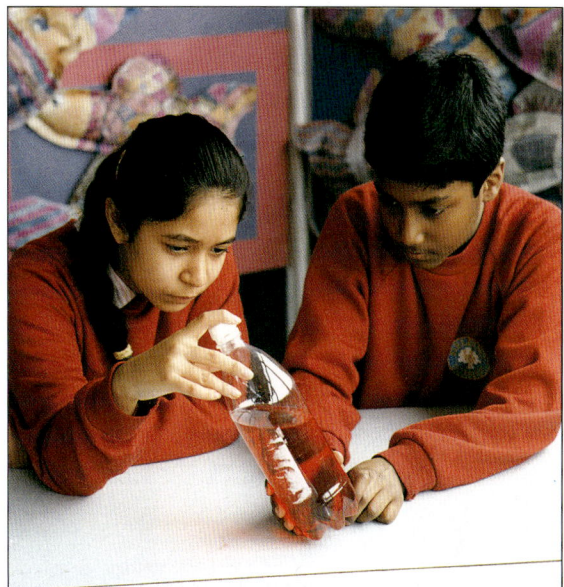

Tip one of the containers like this child. Draw what you see.
Try different containers and tipping them a lot, then a little. What happens to the water levels each time? Use drawings to show what happens.

## OTHER IDEAS

Water is often found under the ground. Some people use sticks or rods called dowsing rods to find it. Try making some dowsing rods like these. Hold them lightly in your hands. Try them in different places. Do they work?

# 2 MOVING LIQUIDS

All liquids flow but some flow quicker than others.
This boy is making gingerbread. He is pouring some
milk and some treacle into a bowl.
Which liquid do you think will pour quicker?

## Liquids move fast or slowly

Different liquids (e.g. cooking oil, fruit juice, treacle, glue) •
your own ideas

These children are using
a board covered with
paper to time how long
it takes for different
liquids to run down it.
They are using a
spoonful of each liquid.

**ACTIVITY – A –**

Plan a test to show which liquids move the quickest.
Think about how you will make it fair.
Collect the things you need.
Make a list of your liquids in the order of how quickly you
think they will flow. Carry out your test.
Did you have any surprises? Why do you think that some
liquids flow quicker than others?
How will you show your results?

Gravity makes liquids flow downwards. If you spill a glass of milk on the table it will pour off the edge onto the floor.
Can you say why:

▶ the taps are above the sink?
▶ the house gutters slope downwards?
▶ the shower is fixed high on the wall?

Think of some more ways that we use water flowing downwards.

## The effect of gravity on liquids

COLLECT

2 water containers • a piece of clean tubing

This woman is filling wine bottles from a big jar. She is using a *siphon* to move the wine. As she sucks the air out of the tube, the wine is forced into the tube. Gravity then makes the wine move from the jar to the bottles.

ACTIVITY
– A –

Fill one container with water. Put the full container on a table and an empty one on the floor. Put one end of the tubing into the water in the full container. Suck the water into the tubing and then put it into the empty container. What happens?

Find out what happens if:

▶ the containers are both on the table?
▶ the containers are both on the floor?
▶ the empty container is placed higher than the full one?

Can you say why the water moves sometimes and not others?
Find a way to show your results.

# 3 EVAPORATION

Have you ever wondered where a puddle goes on a sunny day? As the sun shines, it heats the puddle. Some of the water dries up into the air. The water has changed to water *vapour* and the puddle disappears. When a liquid turns into a vapour or a gas, we say that it has evaporated.

## Investigating evaporation

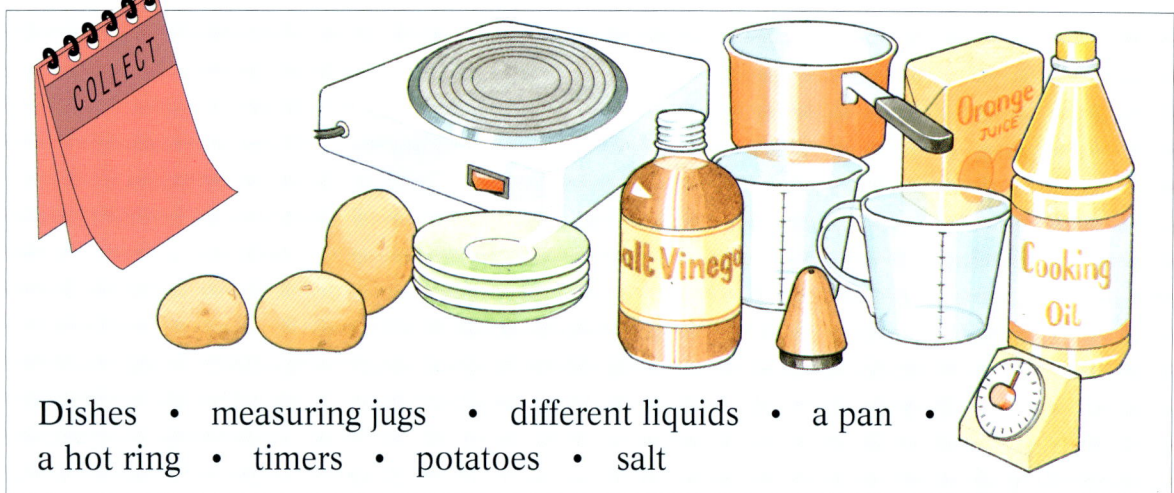

COLLECT

Dishes • measuring jugs • different liquids • a pan • a hot ring • timers • potatoes • salt

ACTIVITY
– A –

Can you find out:
▶ if all liquids evaporate?
▶ if some liquids evaporate quicker than others?
▶ or your own ideas.

These children have measured the same amount of water, oil, vinegar and salty water into 4 separate dishes. They are putting their dishes on a sunny window sill. They will measure how much liquid is left every morning and afternoon and fill in a chart to show their results.
Plan your investigation. Say what you think will happen.
Carry out your investigation. What do you discover?

Be careful with hot water.
Measure some water into the pan.
Heat the water for 3 minutes.
Let the water cool and then measure it again.
Can you say what has happened to the water?

Measure the same amount of water into the pan as you did for Activity B. Add some very small pieces of potato and heat the water for 3 minutes. When it is cool, strain the water off and measure it. What do you notice now?
Some of the water has evaporated and some has been soaked up by the potatoes. How can you find out how much has been evaporated and how much has been soaked up?

If too much water evaporates in cooking the food may dry up or burn so people try to stop too much steam escaping. Plan an investigation to find ways of stopping water evaporating in cooking.
Talk to your teacher about your plan.
Carry out your investigation and show your results.

# 4 CONDENSATION

Have you ever noticed how windows mist up on a cold day?

When people breathe out, the water in the warm air meets the cold glass of the windows. The water vapour in the breath turns back into water. You can often see drops of water running down the windows. When a vapour or a gas turns back into a liquid, we say that it has condensed.

## Misting up

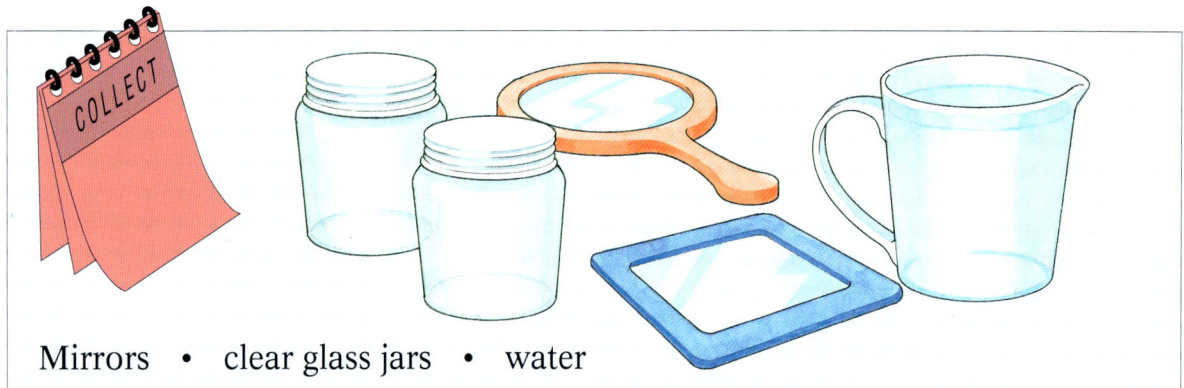

Mirrors • clear glass jars • water

**ACTIVITY – A –**

Breathe on a mirror. What do you notice? You can probably see a misty picture of yourself. Try putting a mirror in a fridge for 10 minutes. Breathe on it again. What do you notice now?

**ACTIVITY – B –**

Half-fill a jar with water. Put it in the fridge for half an hour.
Take it out and watch carefully.
Write down what happens. Can you say why this happens?

# Water in the air

When water in puddles, rivers, lakes and seas evaporates in the warm sun, it rises into the air as water vapour. As it rises, it gets colder. When the water vapour cools down it condenses into water droplets which we see as clouds. Clouds are made from millions of droplets. Sometimes these droplets come together to make bigger drops and then they fall as drops of rain.

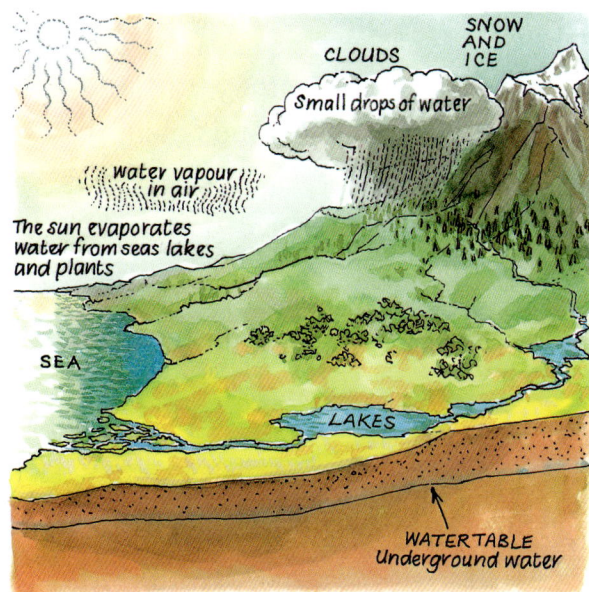

Can you draw a picture story like this one to show how a raindrop is made?

When the water vapour cools near the ground we get foggy weather. Fog and mist are just clouds near the ground. If the water vapour cools down even more at night it condenses to water. We see this as dew on the grass. When the air is very cold the dew is frozen as tiny crystals of ice. We call this frost.

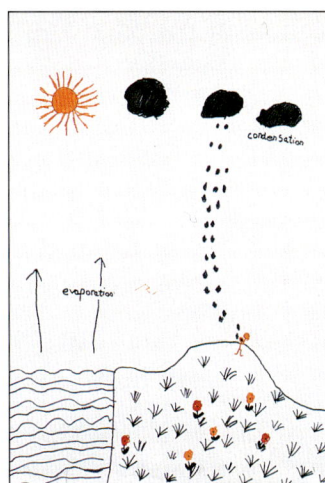

## ACTIVITY

Can you say what is happening in these pictures? Use the words evaporation and condensation to talk about what you see.

## OTHER IDEAS

As water evaporates it cools things down. When your body gets hot it sweats. The sweat evaporates and cools the body down. Can you say why runners put on warm tracksuits after they have raced?

# 5 CHANGING LIQUIDS

When liquids freeze they turn into solids. Water turns into ice.
Ice is a solid. When solids melt, they turn back into liquids.

## Freezing liquids

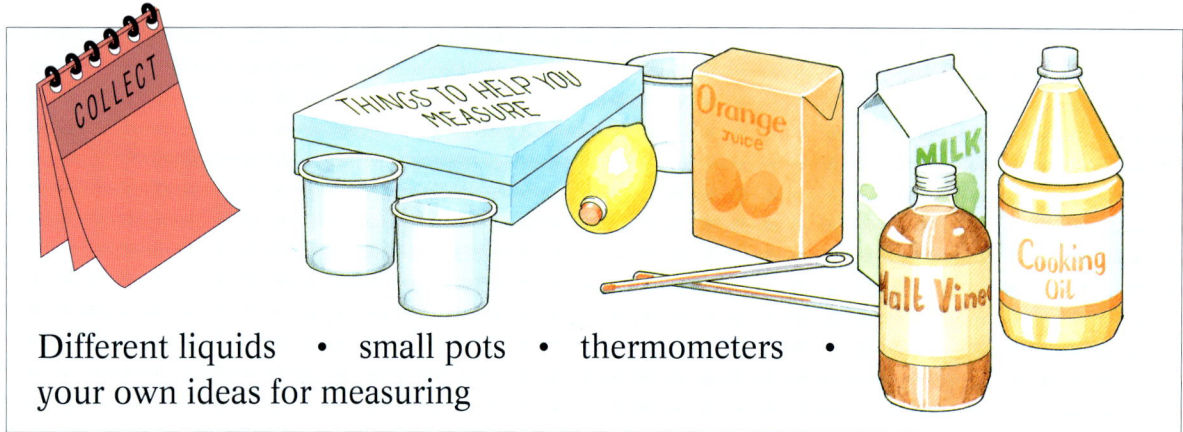

COLLECT

THINGS TO HELP YOU MEASURE

Orange Juice

MILK

Malt Vinegar

Cooking Oil

Different liquids • small pots • thermometers • your own ideas for measuring

**ACTIVITY – A –**

Measure some different liquids into pots. Use one pot for each liquid and use the same amount of each liquid.
Look at them carefully. Write down which of the liquids you think will freeze the quickest and why.
Put your pots in the ice box of a fridge.
Which liquids froze first? Which took longest?

**ACTIVITY – B –**

Some children have found out about the temperatures at which different liquids start to freeze. They made a chart like this to fill in, before they started.
Plan and carry out your own investigation.
Make a bar chart to show your results.
What can you say about your results?

| Liquid | temperature at which it began to freeze |
|---|---|
| Milk | |
| Water | |
| salt water | |
| cooking oil | |

**OTHER IDEAS**

Plan a fair test to find out if a larger amount of liquid takes longer to freeze and melt than a smaller amount.

# Melting from a solid to a liquid

Sometimes we want ice to melt quickly.

In icy weather this lorry spreads a salt mixture on the roads to stop them from freezing over.
Drivers can use a special spray called a de-icer to melt the ice on their car windows.

**COLLECT**

**YOUR OWN IDEAS**

**De-icer**

**ANTI-ICE**

Ice cubes (in a vacuum flask) •
de-icing car sprays • salt • your own ideas

**ACTIVITY**

Use the de-icers outside and always point them away from other people.

Plan a test to find out if salt melts an ice cube more quickly than a de-icer spray.
Think about how you will make your test fair. Will you:

▶ use the same size of ice cubes?
▶ need to time or measure?
▶ do all your tests in the same place?

Write down your test plans and show them to your teacher.
Carry out your test.

**RECORD**

Make a record of your results.
Which way was the quickest? How could you use your ideas?

# 6 MIXING THINGS

When you drink a glass of lemonade or cola, you are drinking a solution. A solution is a mixture of two or more things that look like one thing. Cola looks like a single liquid but really it is a mixture of water, sugar, flavourings and colourings.

## Making a solution

COLLECT

YOUR OWN IDEAS

Different food powders (custard powder, flour, coffee, cocoa, sugar)  •  thermometers  •  small jars  •  timers  •  your own ideas  •  spoons

ACTIVITY

A solution looks like a single liquid because one or more things have been *dissolved* in it. Lots of the things we eat or drink are solutions.

Plan an investigation to find out about the powders in your collection.
You could find out:

▶  if all the powders dissolve to make solutions
▶  how quickly the different powders dissolve to make solutions
▶  if any of the powders dissolve more quickly at higher temperatures.

Make sure that your investigations are fair.
Make a chart to show your results before you start.
Carry out your investigations and record your results.

# Things in liquids

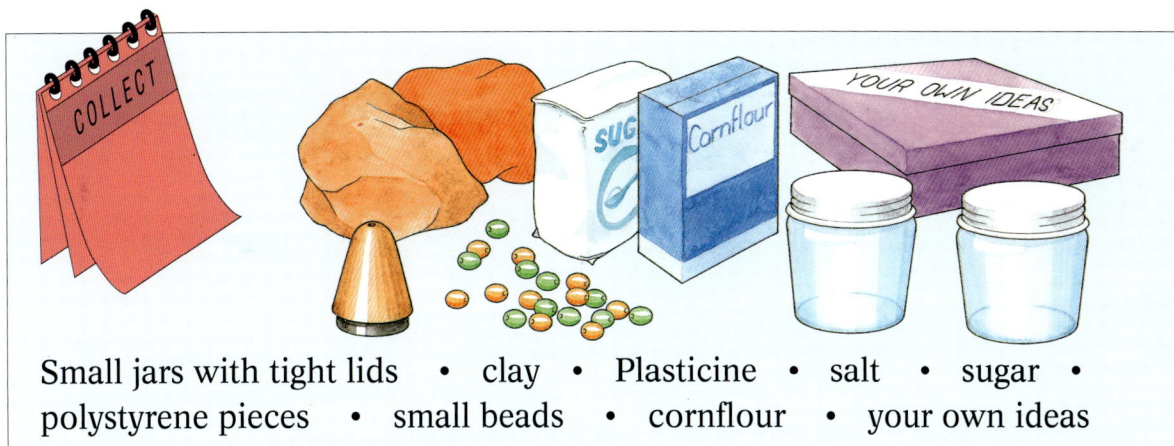

Small jars with tight lids • clay • Plasticine • salt • sugar •
polystyrene pieces • small beads • cornflour • your own ideas

When things are mixed with liquids they may:

▶ float

▶ sink

▶ or dissolve.

Sometimes pieces stay floating in the liquid, like some of the soil in this jar. We say that the pieces are suspended.

**ACTIVITY**

Collect some different things for your investigation. Make a chart like the one here. Use the words: floated, sank, dissolved and suspended.

Shake each thing in a jar of water and leave it to settle. Look at each one and fill in your chart. Did you have any surprises?

| things I used | what happened |
|---|---|
| Clay | Suspended |
| Salt | dissolved Slowly |
| Sugar | Suspended then dissolved |
| beads | floated |
| Rice | suspended then Sank |
| Coconut | Suspended |
| Plasticine | Sank |
| Sand | Suspended than Sank |
| Soil | Suspended |

**OTHER IDEAS**

Plan and carry out an investigation to find out about mixing different liquids.

# Index